Prayers for a Lifestyle of Learning

A 31 Day Devotional for Homeschooling Moms

PAT FENNER

EAGLE WING BOOKS

Prayers for a Lifestyle of Learning: A 31-day Devotional for Homeschool Moms

Printed in the United States of America

ISBN: 978-0-9988226-9-3

Learn more information at BreakthroughHomeschooling.com and www.leggybird.com
Published by Eagle Wings Books
Design Services: Jonathan Lewis/Jonlin Creative

Dedication

There are so very many people that made this particular book possible and for whom I am eternally grateful: my blogging buddy and fellow word-nerd Candy and my longtime friend, Ginny, for their encouragement; my sweet mother-in-law, Pat, who lovingly proofread and suggested clarifications; my husband Paul, who worked with me on content; my five children, who both bless me and bring me to the Cross daily, and my new friend and fellow author, Pam, who helped me keep my nose to the grindstone and get this published.

Most of all, my heart is full of gratitude to the One Who is my rock and Redeemer, and the source for anything I am ever able to accomplish. I could go on for a lifetime about God's grace and mercy in my life and only scratch the surface.

Te Deum

FREE AUDIOBOOK!

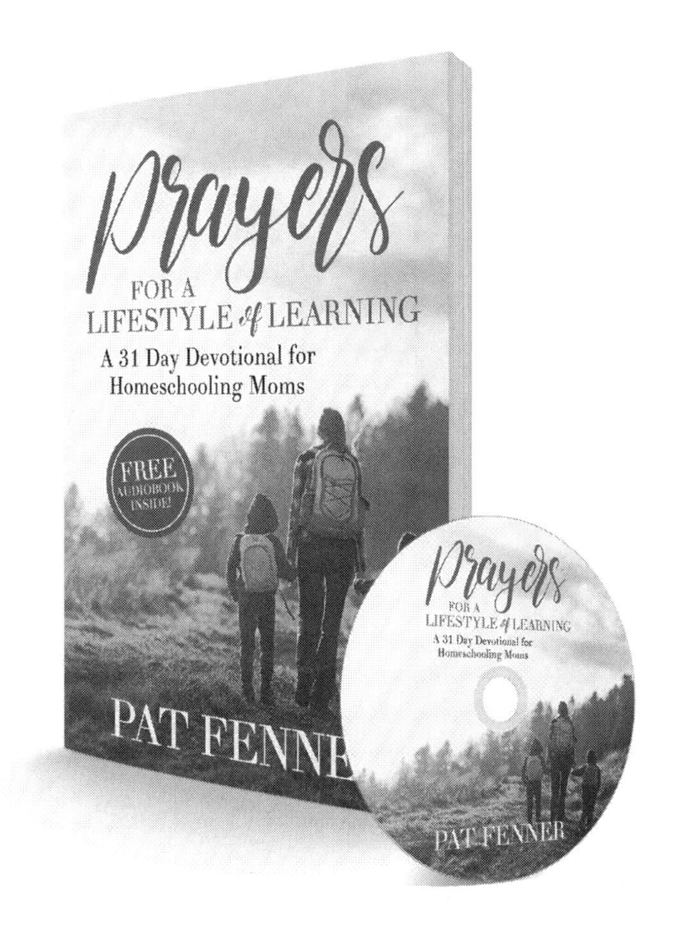

As a thank-you for reading my book, I would like to give you the audiobook version completely free! Just visit the link below to download your copy!

https://breakthroughhomeschooling/freeaudiodevo

NOW IT'S YOUR TURN

Discover the EXACT 3-step blueprint you need to become a bestselling author in 3 months.

Self-Publishing School helped me, and now I want them to help you with this FREE WEBINAR!

Even if you're busy, bad at writing, or don't know where to start, you CAN write a bestseller and build your best life.

With tools and experience across a variety niches and professions, Self-Publishing School is the only resource you need to take your book to the finish line!

DON'T WAIT

Watch this FREE WEBINAR now, and say "YES" to becoming a bestseller:

https://xe172.isrefer.com/go/affegwebinar/bookbrosinc7493/

Contents

Introduction

One day many years ago, while I was still in the midst of a busy homeschool day, I realized that something was missing. I talked to fellow homeschool friends (both online and in real life) and investigated new curricula, believing that the "something" was related to "school"... and then it hit me: I was too focused on being "the source" for our homeschool, and my tank was quickly running dry!

On a quiet morning soon after, while our teens were out volunteering, I managed to "fit in" my quiet time, and the Lord spoke loud and clear: THIS is what's missing - regular time spent in one-on-one communication with the God of the universe Who holds me gently in His hand. He wasn't mad at me, but He made it clear that He had so much to share with me, and that I needed our time together. So I started writing down my concerns and fears and worries, and then searching the Bible to see what He had to say about them. And this little devotional was born.

Today I present it to you, not as a challenge, but as a reminder that you are NOT homeschooling alone; that you are indeed on a mission from the Lord, and that He is for you and wishes to bless your efforts and your family.

Use this book in any way you see fit:

- alongside your Bible reading during your quiet time to refocus your thoughts, or

- helping you work through moments of frustration, fear, and worry, or
- as a gentle reminder, as God used it for me.

He loves you. He loves your children even more than you do. He is an ever-present help in times of trouble. And He is the source of all that brings you joy.

As a homeschool veteran of over 20 years, I've prayed through the concepts in this book time and time again. Hundreds of readers on my blog, who have worked through these concepts when first presented as a 31-day, beginning-of-the-year prayer challenge, have already benefited from them as well.

I know you may feel that you don't have time right now to read this book...that life is too busy as it is and you just can't add one. more. thing. But let me share with you a quick word of caution: if that's what your life is like right now, you may very well be on the road to burnout. Even today you may be frustrated with yourself, your kids, or your curriculum. And if your days are characterized by irritability, a short-temper, and even outright anger, let me encourage you that it doesn't have to be that way!

Working through this devotional can change you from the inside out. Although I don't promise perfection, by the end of this book, I can promise that you'll discover a new sense of calm, an inner peace that comes with knowing you're not the source of everything for your homeschool, and contentment and satisfaction that God is overseeing your efforts and will redeem them for His glory.

The thoughts and prayers in this book center around 5 themes.

I have ordered them in the way I believe our homeschools can best be served. I went through many years, as many homeschool moms do, believing that serving my family came first and then I was somewhere after that. Assuming, of course, that I had any energy or time left over. And sadly, there were many years, especially during those early days with little ones running around, that I only found fleeting moments now and then to squeeze in time for God. But I thank Him that He showed me a better way; His way.

One - Praise and Revival - In all things, Christians are called to serve and glorify God. That concept speaks to the very nature of why we were created. (I Cor 8:6) By asking God to be the builder of our lives and of our homeschools, it follows, then, that we start by giving Him praise.

Two - Seeking Wisdom - As Solomon sought wisdom from the Lord, we move on to asking God for the same. While the prayers are coming from a personal "first person" perspective, let me encourage you to pray the same prayers for wisdom for your husband, the co-teacher in your classroom.

Three - Praying for Ourselves - Praying for ourselves may feel awkward, but it is imperative that we ask God for personal revelation and revival (especially on "those" days...) in order to be the best versions of ourselves and meet all the responsibilities we have (Romans 12:7). (Hint: Staying connected and in-tune with Jesus will allow you to find wisdom about balancing them.)

Four - Praying for Our Family - The fact that we have a family is what makes us parents and brings you here to this book. I hope that praying for them will become as natural to you as breathing, if it isn't already. Showing them how you pray in all things (1 Thes 5:16-18) is a wonderful way to teach your children to do the same.

Five - Praying for Our Homeschools - Which brings us to the last section, the "point" of this book: praying for your homeschool. It might seem a bit strange that I'm leaving this section for last, but I hope you're beginning to see why. For the believer, our homeschool can and should be a natural outgrowth of our faith in God, and our desire to follow and obey Him. Homeschooling is so much more than simply educating our children in worldly subject matter; it is discipling little ones, loving them into the kingdom, and helping them become your brothers and sisters in the Lord. What an awesome blessing and privilege!

On a more-practical note, for each day in this book there is a

Scripture verse, short discussion of the daily topic, and a journal/ prayer prompt. You'll notice that there are sections where you can include the names of your family and/or specific issues you're already praying about, when applicable. (And if you haven't done so already, download the free, printable workbook created especially for this devotional. Grab the link in the Resource section.)

On a special note, the images in this book are all courtesy of my beloved daughter-in-love, Julia Fenner. She is a gifted photographer, and was very generous in sharing her work with me.

I know you're busy, so the length of these devotions is just enough to focus your heart, renew your mind, and keep your eyes on the prize.

It is my prayer that they will strengthen and sustain you as God did me during the 23 years we homeschooled.

Theme 1

GIVING PRAISE AND SEEKING REVIVAL

As a foundation for this study, we begin by focusing on how great God is, and ask Him to forgive our sins and renew our hearts.

Concept 1

We Were Created to Praise God

Come and hear, all you who fear God; let me tell you what he has done for me.
I cried out to him with my mouth;
his praise was on my tongue.
If I had cherished sin in my heart,
the Lord would not have listened;
but God has surely listened
and has heard my prayer.
Praise be to God,
who has not rejected my prayer or withheld his love from me!

Psalm 66:16-20

"Ugh…" It's 5 am and the alarm just went off. Even though it was set to a musical tone, well…it is STILL an alarm.

We've been homeschooling for a loooong time, and the day we "go back to school" after a long holiday is never easy. That's even with homeschooling year 'round; I try to avoid extra-long breaks, because, as I said, the day we "go back…"

It's the same thing when we first start the school year. Tons of fun (for me, at any rate) in the preparation, but not-so-much in the day-to-day implementation.

But I have discovered that it is exactly those times when I need to praise Him.

Not that God needs me to tell Him how wonderful He is, of course. But in His wisdom and mercy, He knows that ***I*** need to tell him that!

Prayer changes things - and most of all, it changes me!

Prayer

Father God, as we start a new day of homeschooling, I want to thank You for Your mercy and goodness. Day by day I'm just blown away by Your kindness and faithfulness. Help me today, Lord, to dwell on the ways you've shown Yourself in my life: the prayers You've answered, the rough times You've walked me through, the faithfulness You've shown *even when I haven't been faithful. (Insert specific examples from your own life here.)* Help me to feel your presence today, God; You know me best, and what it "takes" for me to know that You are with me. Help me to walk with my eyes and heart open - waiting on You and waiting for You. In Jesus' name, Amen.

Dig Deeper

To further "dig in" and deepen your own faith and growth, grab your journal and write a few thoughts to wrap up your time. If you're new to journaling or don't have one, I've created one to accompany this book as a special "Thank you" for your purchase! Access it here: https://breakthroughhomeschooling.com/devojournal

Concept 2

His Greatness is to Be Sought

Praise be to the name of God for ever and ever;
wisdom and power are his.
He changes times and seasons;
he deposes kings and raises up others.
He gives wisdom to the wise
and knowledge to the discerning.
He reveals deep and hidden things;
he knows what lies in darkness,
and light dwells with him.
I thank and praise you…

DANIEL 9:20-23

If we take the time and are truly honest, we can admit that God often has answers that elude us. Whether it's about our kids' behavior, or an issue with our spouse or a friend, or making a curriculum choice, we don't have to fear.

We can praise God that He does have the answer. We can praise

God that He knows what it is - to whatever the question - before we have even formed it in our minds.

He also promises to reveal it, but in His own time.

Meanwhile, we can trust Him. Trust that He knows what is deep and hidden, what lies in darkness, and will that He will bring His light wherever we need it.

Yes, we can thank and praise Him throughout the whole process.

Prayer

All-knowing Father, I greet you this morning at the beginning of a journey. A journey of discovering the depth and breadth of Your love for me, and for my family.

As I continue on, I pray that You will reveal things to me that will cause my hope in You, my trust in You, and my love for You to grow deeper still.

You know the specific situations that I and/or my family if in the middle of, especially *(your own examples here).*

Even without knowing what the future holds, loving God, I'm thanking and praising you this day, and each one to come. In Jesus' name, Amen.

Concept 3

Praise Him for His Omniscience

Praise the Lord.
How good it is to sing praises to our God, how pleasant and fitting to praise him! The Lord builds up Jerusalem; he gathers the exiles of Israel. He heals the brokenhearted and binds up their wounds.
He determines the number of the stars and calls them each by name.
Great is our Lord and mighty in power; his understanding has no limit.
The Lord sustains the humble
but casts the wicked to the ground.

Psalm 147:1-6

Do you know how many stars are in the sky? Google estimates there are 100 billion starts in our Milky Way galaxy. But even the smartest astronomer, or a NASA scientist, would be quick to say that the exact number is not known.

The same goes with how many hairs are on your head and mine: we may not know, but He does!

Think about it: our God can do so many things that we can't. How many exiles of a nation have **you** gathered together? Whose hearts have **you** been able to heal? Not make them feel a bit better, or calm them down, but heal? Do **you** know how many stars there are - and even more, their names? Do you consider yourself mighty in power, or possessing limitless understanding or knowledge?

Yes, you may laugh at the questions, but you have to admit that many of us often act is if we were:

- able to control others...
- able to heal…
- mighty in power…
- without limits to our understanding…

Let's leave the "all-knowing" to God - in our lives and in our homeschools!

Prayer

All-knowing God, you have not only created the universe, but You know exactly what it needs to keep going! Your knowledge extends to everything that I do know…and far beyond. I praise You, God, that there is nothing out of Your consciousness. That You know everything from the names and number of stars in the sky… to the number of hairs on my head, and the thoughts in my heart.

Lord, as we prepare to begin a new school day, I beg for Your wisdom, Your power, and Your presence to blanket my family. Fill our days with learning about the wonderful world You created, as our hearts grow in Your wisdom. In Jesus' name I pray, Amen.

Concept 4

We Lift Our Hands to Praise God

Arise, cry out in the night, as the watches of the night begin;
pour out your heart like water in the presence of the Lord.
Lift up your hands to him for the lives of your children,

LAMENTATIONS 2:19

Although I was raised Catholic, most of my married life has been spent in small, non-denominational, charismatic-leaning churches. Raising hands in praise is not new to me, and is something I've become quite comfortable with.

But there's another, little-considered, benefit to raising hands in praise.

I discovered it one morning, shortly after I'd read something about the health benefits to many of the dietary rules in the Old Testament. With no refrigeration and poor sanitary conditions, God was also looking out for His people's physical health when He told them what to eat and what not to eat!

And lifting our hands in praise is good for our health, too! Did you know that?

Try this one today: When you first swing your feet off the bed, sit up straight and tall, reach for the sky, and say "Good Morning!" to Jesus. Continue to praise Him as your reach up with both hands, then as you kind of "climb" up a wall. As you slowly stand up, continue to reach up. Lower your hands and take a few deep breaths, and then sing or hum a favorite worship tune. As you do so, circle your shoulders and arms and finish the song with your hands held high again, and your face looking up to the sky (I like to close my eyes at this point, too).

When we raise our hands we're opening up our diaphragm, allowing more oxygen to enter our lungs and our brain. This enables us to wake up, think more clearly, and get a great start to our day.

With God's help, our hearts and minds are now ready to face whatever life throws at us!

Prayer

Good morning, Father God! As I lift up my hands to You today, let me again praise You for Who You are! As this day goes by, Lord, help me to never stop pouring out my heart to You. Let me take each thought captive: each joy, each problem, every frustration, and lift them up to You. As I think of or interact with my husband and my children, with any member of my family and my friends, let me remember that You love them and care deeply for us all. Forgive my frustrations and poor decisions and yes, sins, this day; allow me to accept Your forgiveness and live eternally grateful for Your mercy.

I also lift up my child/ren to you by name: ____________. Help me to remember that as much as I love them, you love them even more! In Jesus' name, Amen.

Concept 5

His Joy is Our Strength

Create in me a pure heart, O God,
and renew a steadfast spirit within me.
Do not cast me from your presence or take your Holy Spirit from me.
Restore to me the joy of your salvation and grant me a willing spirit, to sustain me.

Psalm 51:10-12

Do you know the song "The Joy of the Lord is My Strength"? It was one of the first Scripture songs that my two oldest children and I learned. I found it on a cassette tape (yes, it was that long ago!) and since they loved music, and I wanted to learn Scripture along with them, we listened to it endlessly in the car.

Later on in life, when I discovered Keith Green, we all enjoyed his recording of the song "Create in Me a Clean Heart".

Both of those songs refer to the joy that only comes from knowing - really knowing - the Lord, and all that He does for us.

Do you have that joy in your heart? Do you know the salvation that comes from God? Have you allowed Him to create a pure heart inside you? This kind of joy makes all the difference.

It makes all the difference when things aren't going well at home. When there are health problems or financial problems looming over your head. When you are in a situation that seems hopeless and without an acceptable solution.

You know, He alone is the source of unspeakable joy. And He is willing and able and even yearns to share that with you! Today, and every day.

Prayer

Jesus, this morning I praise You as the source of joy and hope in every day and situation and place I find myself. I come to You this morning with all my frailties and imperfections and shortcomings, and ask that You would take them all and replace them with Your joy. *(Insert a specific personal challenge that is troubling you today.)* Help me to know that nothing will happen to me today that hasn't first been sifted through Your loving hands. You alone provide all the strength I will ever need, and that in You I can find joy to meet anything that life throws at me. Create in me this day a pure heart and a right spirit that will worship and serve You in every situation. In Jesus' name, I pray, Amen.

Concept 6

What Does it Take to Bring Revival?

For this is what the high and exalted One says—he who lives forever, whose name is holy: "I live in a high and holy place, but also with the one who is contrite and lowly in spirit, to revive the spirit of the lowly and to revive the heart of the contrite.

ISAIAH 57:15

Revival is a word often bantered about in religious circles. I say "bantered" because it is often a buzz word for a purely emotional experience; something that "feels good" but has no lasting substance.

I love this definition of revival: "a restoration to bodily or mental vigor, to life or consciousness." True revival requires us to lay down our own lives: our dreams and hopes, our human desires and sins, and do a 180. This repentance lays the groundwork, and the ensuing revival is what enables us to feel the joy of the Lord in our hearts and be completely restored. As that vigor spills over into our lives... well, the transformation it can make is nothing short of miraculous!

Because you're reading this, it's obvious that God has laid revival on your heart in some form or fashion. Spend some time with Him today, asking Him to do what it takes to bring true revival to your life. Then stay out of the way...and watch what happens!

Prayer

Holy Deliverer, Lord of all, You bring revival and renewal to all who put their trust and faith in You. I come to You this morning, seeking the rebirth and new life that only You can bring. Show me in Your perfect way what roadblocks are in my life right now. Encourage me, Lord, and bring joy to my heart as You bring revival to my heart; turn this situation around *(name yours here)* so that I may once again feel the joy of Your presence. I so need revival in this area! Prick my conscience, God, so that I can discover the sins and attitudes and actions that I need to repent of, and by doing so lay the groundwork for a move of Your Spirit.

God, there is nothing that hurts my heart more than knowing how my sin has hurt Your Son. And my prayer is that I would be able to lead the young ones You've blessed me with in Your ways. So heal me of my sin, help me to turn and walk in Your ways, keep my feet sure on Your paths, and let me be the salt and light that You desire me to be in the world around me. In Jesus' name I pray, Amen.

Concept 7
God is Sovereign

Though the fig tree does not bud and there are no grapes on the vines,
Though the olive crop fails and the fields produce no food,
Though there are no sheep in the pen and no cattle in the stalls,
Yet I will rejoice in the Lord, I will be joyful in God my Savior.

HABAKKUK 3:17-18

Many times we are tempted to question all the suffering and cruelty in the world. My children have asked about it as they've grown, and I wonder about it sometimes, too.

Related to our homeschool, I've also wondered why God allows us to walk through seasons of trial, whether they're problems with our kids, mounting bills, poor health, marriage issues, etc. It is during those times that I am tempted to rail my fist at God. Yes, the Creator of the Universe.

But then I am reminded that the life of a believer is NOT a guarantee of ease, but a guarantee of grace, and it is then that I can echo the words of the prophet Habakkuk.

Friend, sometimes your curriculum will be a dud, there will be times when there are no funds to go on that interesting field trip or take a class that you think would be just great for the kids. There may be times when you'll have to take a job (at home or outside the home) and balance yet another "hat" and set of responsibilities. There may be times when you'll look at another homeschooling family who seems to have all they want and be "living the life", and wonder what's wrong with your life, or what you did or are doing wrong.

Even if you're not feelin' it, commit **today** to "rejoice in the Lord" **then,** and trust that He will bring all things together in the end. Trust also that He will be right beside you, comforting you and giving direction when you ask.

Prayer

Sovereign God, I come to you today wanting to rejoice in my heart, and with a desire to trust You at all times. Even though things may not be going well, please help me to keep my eyes on You always, and remember that nothing goes unnoticed. *(Insert a specific situation you're struggling with right now.)* You are a God of both judgment and mercy, and my heart's desire is to wait patiently for You. In Your sovereignty, I lift up this day, and all that I think and do and say, to Your everlasting Name. The troubles and cares of this day are fleeting, but You, Lord, are forever... In Jesus' name, Amen.

Theme 2

SEEKING WISDOM

Scripture tells us that true wisdom comes from using our skills, gifts, and the knowledge we acquire to give God glory. In this section, we are seeking wisdom for ourselves, and asking God to show us how to lead and disciple our children in ways that are pleasing to Him.

Concept 8

It All Starts with Fear (Awe) of the Lord

The fear of the Lord is the beginning of knowledge, but fools despise wisdom and instruction.

Proverbs 1:7

There's almost nothing more irritating than a fool. You know what I'm talking about. The person (or people?) in our lives who is uber-sure that they have the answer; the one who has to have the last word; the one who looks down condescendingly at everyone else around him. It's hard to be around that type of person. And yet that person is sometimes facing you in the mirror!

Even when we're confident that we're hearing from the Lord, it's important to remember that our hearts are deceitful. And because of that, we, too, are prone to pridefully thinking we know it all. It can make itself clear in our attitudes or thoughts, or the way we treat or react to others.

The best way to teach our children, of course, is to model the particular character trait or behavior we're desiring to grow in them. So be ever-attentive to your approach, mom: to the day, to learning, to correction, to a change in plans, to disappointment, to hurt, to offense. Of course, it's just as important that we're not overly harsh on ourselves when (not if) we fail. Being forgiving starts with forgiving ourselves, and it's very likely one of the hardest things many of us will learn. And being ever-mindful or in awe of the Lord does not mean that we are afraid of Him, but that we submit to His will, that we are conscious of His wisdom and omniscience, and move forward confident that He knows best and has our best at heart.

So, to review:

- practice what you preach
- forgive yourself when you fail
- stay open and in-tune to God's wisdom and instruction

Now let's be open to wisdom and instruction in the same way we're open to receiving outright blessings!

Prayer

Awesome God, ugh, it pains my heart, and well, embarrasses me to think that I sometimes take the appearance of a fool. I know in my head that You are the author and finisher of my faith and my life, the creator of the universe with wisdom and knowledge above all. And yet...

Lord, please forgive me when I assume I know best, when I assume that You are too busy or unconcerned or not involved in my life. Help me to run to you first in all things, especially regarding *(your specific situation here)*. Help my life to have the qualities and characteristics that bring You joy and serve You well. Allow my children to see and copy that behavior, too, and, in doing so,

Lord, turn their hearts to You. May they seek after Your wisdom and instruction all the days of their lives. I pray this in the name of Jesus, Amen.

Concept 9

Our Faith Grows in and from God's Power

My message and my preaching were not with wise and persuasive words,
but with a demonstration of the Spirit's power,
so that your faith might not rest on human wisdom, but on God's power.
We do, however, speak a message of wisdom among the mature,
but not the wisdom of this age or of the rulers of this age, who are coming to nothing.

1 Corinthians 2:4-6

When our oldest daughter was about 2, she suffered an attack of acute glomerulonephritis. Basically, for no reason we could ever discern, her kidneys shut down. We were living in a tiny village outside the capital of Guatemala, with limited access to healthcare and little understanding of Spanish. On top of it all, this experience reminded me how my own mother had died when I was little: as a result of chronic kidney failure.

To say I was freaking out is an understatement. I. was. a. mess. I was also not exactly a great example for our kids of living in faith and trusting in God's power.

We asked for earnest prayer from our family and friends and were able to get local medical care. By the time we returned to the States, the doctors at the highly-esteemed children's hospital we admitted her to declared she was already healed. Still recuperating, yes, but there was nothing medically wrong with her.

It was a lesson in humility and gratitude.

It was a lesson in resting on God's power.

It was a lesson in growing my faith in how GOD could take care of me and those I love.

The experience was terrifying. It would be easy for me to rail at God and complain about how He had allowed her illness to happen. And, to be honest, I did go through a period when I did. But I chose, through God's grace and my husband's loving encouragement, to move forward and use the opportunity to grow my faith in His abilities to heal and walk us through a fear-filled valley.

Prayer

Jehova Rapha, my healer, thank you for Your powerful ability to heal and to carry me through situations in which I feel totally hopeless. Help me to grow my faith by trusting in Your power, by humbly seeking and accepting Your healing touch, and by learning to rest in all that entails. I know that my abilities and strength are so limited, Lord, and yet I fight against Your plan and purposes, which leads me away from You. Heal my body from sickness and disease. But even more so, heal my heart and open my eyes to see Your work in this world and in my life. And in the process, help my faith grow deeper and stronger each day. Today, Lord, I also lift up *(insert family member's name here, health situation, and your request)*. I pray this in the name of Jesus, Amen.

Concept 10

Ask For, and Expect, Answers Daily

If any of you lacks wisdom, you should ask God,
who gives generously to all without finding fault,
and it will be given to you.

James 1:5

So I say to you: Ask and it will be given to you; seek and you will find;
knock and the door will be opened to you.
For everyone who asks receives; the one who seeks finds;
and to the one who knocks, the door will be opened.

Luke 11:9-10

Where I live there's a nearly-automatic response from church-folk when something is requested of them: "I'll pray about it!" It's almost a joke, in that very often the real message is "I need/want to say 'No', but I can't. So don't wait for a response from me."

Yet, "praying about it" is never a bad idea.

I had "double booked" myself…yet again! I had scheduled a meeting with a new homeschool mom at the same time I had agreed to sub at our children's co-op. I knew that I could reschedule my meeting with a simple phone call, but I was frustrated with myself. I seemed to be saying "Yes" too often, and trying to be all things to all the people in my life.

What I realized was that I wasn't seeking wisdom in my choices. After choosing to spend time with the Lord that morning, I realized I wasn't seeking Him in all things: and first of all, in my schedule. It's easy to give lip service to seeking God's will, but the true question is: how often - or even do you - seek God in your decision-making? Yes, He provides in extreme cases - physical safety in a storm, healing illness, providing for an immediate need. But He is also a God Who has wisdom for every little situation in our lives, and Who is eager to share that wisdom with us!

Whether it's your daily schedule, or a parenting or schooling issue with your child, or troubles with your spouse or a friend, heck, even if it's where to find the best sales that week when you're shopping for groceries, He is there with the wisdom you need when you need it. He's only waiting for you to ask Him.

As I was getting dressed that morning, and preparing to pick up the phone to call the homeschooling mom, the phone rang. She was calling me to reschedule with her because her son woke up sick. I smiled as I sensed God's help, and asked her if I could call her back later in the day. After co-op I came home, spent some time in prayer, looked over my calendar, and picked up the phone. Joy and peace settled in me as we chose a time together. I knew that I was beginning to apply a lesson that was a long time coming.

Prayer

God of all wisdom, there are so many sources of knowledge in this world. So many places to learn facts and figures that, in the end, are mere trivia. What I need to seek each day is the wisdom that comes from You, especially *(insert a specific situation that comes to mind).* What do You have to say about my situation? What do You say I should do or know to stay on the path of righteousness? As I teach my children, help them understand the value of learning, but help them to always look to YOU for wisdom, and find truth and value in Your teaching. This day, and every day, with every lesson we learn, may we find ways to better serve Your people and further Your kingdom. In Jesus' name, Amen.

Concept 11

Listening Brings Favor and Blessing

The complacency of fools will destroy them; but whoever listens to me will live in safety and be at ease, without fear of harm.

PROVERBS 1:32-33

Oh, how I hated my dad's lectures when I was a little girl. They always seemed to come at inconvenient times (like when I was waiting for a friend's phone call, or my favorite TV show was on), and there was never any opportunity for conversation. No discussion, no clarification (and I was often confused by his rambling)...nothing.

Of course, I have to say for my part, there was no humility, no deference for his age or his position as my dad, very little respect for his wisdom or desire to learn from it.

I'm pretty sure that the stage was being set even then for the really stupid things I would do later as a teenager and then young adult. I was smug in my own "wisdom", (over) confident in my abilities, and rarely sought wise counsel. Although I did not live in fear - because I was too ignorant to notice danger or potential harm around me - yeah, I was headed for destruction.

But God… He saw me in my own foolishness, not even yet knowing my need for Him, and saved me anyway! Not a day goes by that I don't thank Him for His mercy toward me, grateful for His saving grace in my life.

And I'm so thankful for the lessons I learned from those days. I'm more aware of those same attitudes in my own kids: smugness, lack of respect, ignorance and unwillingness to listen and learn.

Some people say they don't feel they can correct their kids when they see them make the same mistakes or sins that they themselves have made; that they feel hypocritical. I feel exactly the opposite: why would I want somebody I love to live the same ignorant life I did? Make the same foolish mistakes? Commit the same grievous sins against God?

I know what life is like, but even so, I want my children to live without fear of harm by their own doing.

Prayer

Almighty Father, I pray that You would strengthen in my own heart a continued love for learning, and birth in my children's hearts a desire for growing in Your wisdom, too. Give us all humble hearts as we move forward in life. Allow us to live in safety and be at ease, without fear of harm, knowing that we have Your wisdom and protection as our shield. May nothing that is formed against us prosper, and may we rest peacefully knowing we are in Your care. God, help me to be aware of situations that I need to address in my children's lives, especially *(ask Him about a situation that you're aware of)*. Prick their own conscience and bless them with wisdom about situations that are unknown to me. I love you, Jesus, and offer this day, and all that I do or say, to You.

Concept 12

True Discernment Comes from God

And this is my prayer: that your love may abound more and more in knowledge and depth of insight

PHILIPPIANS 1:9

The baby had just fallen asleep, and my two-year-old wanted to play.

That was often how our afternoons went, except that I had been up most of the previous night with a sick baby, and spent much of the morning at the doctor's office. I was in no mood to play.

In fact, I was downright angry that my two-year-old couldn't see my exhaustion.

I know that sounds silly, but it wasn't at the time… And I didn't handle it well at all. #momfail

Fast forward three children and many years later. I had just settled down for an afternoon nap, trying to relieve a nagging migraine. The kids all had assignments to work on, and they were usually trustworthy, but I was in such pain, I didn't really care what happened anyway. All too soon, my darling youngest daughter was tapping me on the shoulder. "Mom," she whispered, "don't worry about it, Matt helped me clean it all up." Not a good way to wake up, wouldn't you agree?

I shot out of bed (as best I could) and down the hallway to her bedroom to look in the door. It was evident that a decent attempt had been made to clean up the effects from the bottle of red nail polish that had obviously spilled. Ugh. This time, tho, I quickly realized a few things. 1) She was just a child. 2) She did make a rather valient attempt to clean up her own mess. 3) It was "only" a carpet (and not a new or special one at that) and my getting carried away over a childish mistake would certainly damage our relationship, which is special! And 4) she was clearly very sorry about what she had done.

I bent down and hugged her. Reassured her that she and we were ok. And helped her to do a little more clean-up as we talked together about it. #momwin

What was the difference? Years of time spent in the Word and in prayer, lifting my emotions up to the Father, begging for His wisdom and discernment between childishness and sin. Dealing with my own shortcomings and sin. Parenting experience. Reading and seeking wise counsel often.

The result was a more loving mother. By no means a perfect one yet (at least on this side of the grave!), but one who lives and is growing in forgiveness, understanding, and discernment.

Prayer

All-knowing Father, author and source of all wisdom, I pray today that as I grow in knowledge and depth of insight by learning from You through Your Word, that You would grow me into a more loving person. Someone, dear Father, who more and more each day reflects You and Your Son to a dying, lost and sinful world. I pray that as we teach our children at home they might also grow in "wisdom and stature and favor with God and with man", as Jesus did under the loving tutelage of his own earthly parents. Thank you for the privilege and opportunity to educate our children at home. Please help me make the most of every moment of this day, lavishly loving those You send into my life...those through whom You bless me daily!

Concept 13

Becoming Wise Is a Process

For this reason, since the day we heard about you, we have not stopped praying for you. We continually ask God to fill you with the knowledge of his will through all the wisdom and understanding that the Spirit gives, so that you may live a life worthy of the Lord and please him in every way

COLOSSIANS 1:9-10

OK, so, raise your hand: how many of you, while trying to teach your young children to pick up after themselves or to do a simple household chore, periodically gave up in despair and say "Gah! It's just easier to do it myself!"?

Training a child to do a chore, teaching a subject to your student, learning a new skill or job responsibility - even as an adult - is a process.

The definition of process is "a series of actions or steps taken to achieve a particular end." Notice, it says "series of"...not a singular one. It's not a one-time deal.

This also applies to developing wisdom.

We know that one does not wake up one morning and simply

BE wise all of a sudden. To even suggest that probably makes you smile a bit, realizing the foolishness of the suggestion.

But by extension, we not only need to be patient with our children, and then our teens, but also with ourselves and our spouses.

The journey God has us on is just that: a journey. It's similar to a process in that it is a series of steps. With His grace and mercy, we will grow in wisdom as we continue to follow His steps, as we continue to learn from the inevitable mistakes we will make, as we continue to turn to Him in repentance, asking for insight and wisdom.

The Grand Canyon was not crafted in a day. Neither do we become wise souls overnight. Let's keep approaching His throne, day by day, and pray that the Holy Spirit meets us there!

Prayer

All-knowing Father, author and source of all wisdom, I pray today as I grow in knowledge and depth of insight by learning from You through Your Word, that You would grow me into a more wise and loving person. Someone, dear Father, who more and more each day reflects the wisdom that is only available through You and by Your grace. Teach me to be patient with the process, patient with myself and with the blessings you shower on me in the form of my family and friends.

Lord, give me wisdom about my limitations *(insert some known ones here)*, but don't let me become shallow and afraid to grow and try new things. Give me wisdom about my responsibilities, especially *(insert some that are feeling burdensome today)* so that I don't take on that which is too much for me, or not "my job". And finally, give me wisdom about being the wife and parent You created me to be; someone who both nurtures at home and enables my children to be fully capable and free as they leave our nest. I ask all this of you in Jesus' precious name, Amen.

Concept 14

Wisdom Bears Fruit

But the wisdom that comes from heaven is first of all pure; then peace-loving, considerate, submissive, full of mercy and good fruit, impartial and sincere.

James 3:17

My husband has always had a dream of living on a property full of fruit-bearing bushes and trees. (I think it's the secret "farmer" in him.) A long time ago he dreamt that he saw our children playing among grapevines in the yard of a house we lived in. The Father's Day after we moved into our home, the kids and I bought him a handful of grapevines, intent on planting the beginnings of his own personal vineyard. We studied up on what they needed to grow well beforehand (gotta love homeschooling!) and placed them appropriately in the yard. We watered them, fertilized them, and yes, I admit to praying over them (this is because of my well-documented lack of a green thumb, and a past history of what I do to plants). But when Father's Day came, well let's just say we didn't have much to show for our efforts.

Fortunately, however, that's NOT what happens with God's Word! He promises us that it will never return void, which means when we allow it into our hearts through prayer and reading Scripture, it will bear fruit. (Isaiah 55:11). Furthermore, He even describes that fruit for us: love, joy, peace, patience, kindness, goodness, faithfulness, and self-control (Galatians 5:22).

What a gift! We have a loving Father who gives us a picture of what it will look like in our lives as we grow in wisdom... I'm so grateful that ***I'm*** not the gardener!

Prayer

Lord, as we start another day in our homeschool, help me to lean into you as my source of wisdom. Help me to grow, day-by-day, and make my life bear the fruit that comes from learning from You and living my life according to Your wisdom.

Help me realize that there are no shortcuts or tricks to wisdom; there is only You. No matter what this day brings, carry me with Your grace through it. And help me to see the events at opportunities to learn and grow in wisdom on this journey. In Jesus' name I pray, Amen.

Theme 3

PRAYING FOR OURSELVES

I know, I know, those words look odd, don't they? "Praying for Ourselves"

It seems almost "un-Christian" to think about that. I mean, I ***know*** *that God knows what I need, right? That He created me and has a plan for me, has numbered all the hairs on my head and all that.*

And yet, He encourages us to pray for ourselves: to ask for wisdom (James 1:5), to seek His will (Romans 12:2), to repent and seek His forgiveness (Luke 24:47).

Additionally, we can't give what we don't have. And I don't know about you, but there are many times when this ol' pitcher is empty or, worse yet, filled with bitter water. And that certainly leaves me in no condition to serve.

So during these few days, consider covering these areas in prayer for yourself. You don't need to feel guilty about it when you are asking with a pure heart. Ask Him first to show you where you may be lacking, then repent and move on to teaching and serving in grace and freedom!

Concept 15

Returning to Yourself

Then God said, "Let us make man in our image, after our likeness.

GENESIS 1:26

Indeed, the very hairs of your head are all numbered. Don't be afraid; you are worth more than many sparrows

LUKE 12:7

My husband had taken a new job 5 hours from home, and I and the kids had stayed behind to finish up the school year and see kiddo #4 through to high school graduation. Our family had just made a major move out-of-State, and our "baby" was entering high school. She had expressed curiosity about attending the local public school. And according to our realtor and information I could discover, it had a pretty good reputation.

All of a sudden I found myself in new territory. Not only

physically, but emotionally, socially, vocationally, relationally, and probably another "ly" or two that I could think of!

I was left with myself and God - which, of course, is where He wanted me all along!

Now, I wanted to follow His lead about my next step, but although I prayed in earnest, I didn't seem to hear an answer. One day I was bemoaning my fate to my new small group, and asking for prayer, when one of the ladies said something quite remarkable.

"Perhaps He's waiting to hear from YOU."

What she meant was that perhaps it was time to take a personal assessment of the strengths, interests, gifts, and talents that I already possessed, and choose how I would move forward. The only problem with that line of thinking, was that I had to have an idea of those things. "What do you want to do?" she asked.

I didn't have a clue how to answer that. My ignorance and the inner "angst" that ensued, besides a few other life challenges that came my way, led me to personal counseling, where, again, I was asked the same question. While I was still without an answer, my counselor encouraged me to dig into thinking this through.

"It's Biblical", she explained, "to understand how God's wired you and what talents He's gifted you with, so you can fulfill His plan and purpose for you. Don't rush the process of returning to yourself."

And so began a journey that I am still working through today. Trust me, if you make self-discovery and self-care a regular part of your life during the homeschool years, it'll make the years after homeschooling is over that much easier!

Prayer

El Shaddai, all-sufficient God of Heaven, You created me as part of Your plan, with gifts and talents to accomplish what You desire of me. Help me today to discover more of what I'm capable of, in order to be a part of furthering Your kingdom. Then help me to see how to best use those gifts and talents in the situations I will face or am facing *(and share them here)*.

As I encourage my children to spread their wings, help me to do the same Lord, and truly believe that, together with You, I am enough. Help me to say "Yes!" to You, and by doing so, gain the wisdom, strength, and courage to accomplish today what I most fear or doubt I can do *(insert details of your greatest challenge here)*.

I thank you in advance for what You have done and will do in and through me this day, in Jesus' name, Amen.

Concept 16

Renewing Your Mind

Do not conform to the pattern of this world, but be transformed by the renewing of your mind. Then you will be able to test and approve what God's will is—his good, pleasing and perfect will.

ROMANS 12:2

Do you play mind tapes? You know what I mean...those recurring comments that roll around in your head during the day. If we're not careful, they can take the form of thoughts that keep us from being our best selves. They can also be an unhealthy expression of frustration at behaviors that "bug" us: "Why do my kids always fight?", "Why doesn't my hubby ever pick his socks up from the living room floor?", "Gah - lost my temper again...I'm such a lousy mom!"

Those mind tapes may be a reflection of other issues in our lives. We may be looking at activities from a worldly perspective, or developing a bad habit of negativity. But God calls us to a higher standard, and He promises to equip us for whatever He calls us to do. In this verse, He encourages us to renew our minds, promises transformation, and points out how much more effective our lives will be as a result - sounds like a win-win in my book!

These have been some of my less-than-wonderful mind tapes over the years, and how they were "transformed". I hope you can find some encouragement in them.

- "Why can't I seem to find a math curriculum that will work for my son?" became "What a model of perseverance he sees as we explore new learning tools!"
- "Ugh, is THIS what my kids are learning from me?" became "God, please forgive my parenting mistakes and redeem them in my children's lives."
- "I'm not ready to give up homeschooling yet, Lord!" became "Show me how to use this time in a way that glorifies You and blesses others."
- And finally, "I'll never finish this book!" became "Thank you for being with me every step of the way, leading me and lighting up this crazy path!"

Over time and little by little, He has transformed me - He can certainly do the same for you!

Prayer

Heavenly Father, I come to You this morning in awe of Your wisdom and power to transform. Lord, You know my heart, and I ask that as we move forward in learning You would be my source of knowledge and wisdom. Change my mind day by day so that it reflects Your thoughts, Your love, and You. Help me to come to You with every decision I have to make, with every sticky situation I'm in. Whether I'm struggling with discipline issues, curriculum and class choices, or outside commitments and responsibilities, I need Your help with everything! *(insert today's needs here)* May I always leave me with a new and refreshed outlook and plan after time spent with You.

Renew my mind daily so that it is more in line with Your will for me and for our family, and in-tune to how You would have me respond to each situation in which I find myself. Help my children see and imitate that as well, growing in wisdom and grace as they turn to You. I know You're generous to those who ask, and so I come to You asking this in Jesus' name, Amen.

Concept 17

Caring for Your Temple

I praise you, for I am fearfully and wonderfully made. Wonderful are your works; my soul knows it very well.

Psalm 139:14

If there's one thing most homeschooling moms I know don't have, it's time to take care of themselves. At least, that's what we say.

But this final Scripture is a reminder that we are one of God's wonderful works. As we are called to be good stewards of God's gifts and blessings in our lives, that includes being good stewards of ourselves!

So when we neglect self-care activities, even basic ones such as getting enough sleep, eating well, and maintaining our personal hygiene, we're not taking care of one of God's wonderfully-made works.

Stop and think about that for a moment: YOU are fearfully and wonderfully made.

When God looks at you, He thinks about you with a gajillion

times more love than when you look at your children as they sleep. He cares deeply for every aspect of your life, and always has your best interests at heart. You are worth taking care of.

I know it may feel selfish, mom, but try this today: take a few minutes for yourself and write down 5 things you enjoy doing... activities that fill you up. They don't have to be anything remarkable - they just have to work for YOU. And then purpose to do at least one of them this week. Schedule quiet time, have some "me time" at the library (without the kiddos!), meet a friend for coffee, call your sister, get a sitter so you can go on a date with your hubby, schedule a mani/pedi or a haircut. (Those are some "freebies" to get ya' started.)

Learning self-care without being selfish or "me-focused" is one of the greatest lessons we can pass on to our kids. Quite frankly, it may be one of those that is more "caught" than "taught".

So seek God's guidance to make wise choices in this area, ask Him also to help you discern balance, and then confidently move forward to take care of yourself for a change. I guarantee you'll be amazed at and grateful for the blessing!

Prayer

Good morning, good Father! I thank you today for the grace and abilities and strength You've given me as I care for my family. Lord, I thank You for each soul I take care of, but confess to You that I haven't always taken good care of myself.

As You transform my mind daily, help me to see how much I am valued in Your eyes, and help me to be a good steward of my own life. I know that You are my source and my rock, supplying all my needs, even before I may know them. But help me to consider self-care as a stewardship issue, and show me how to extend the same love and concern I show to those in my care...to myself.

Thank You for my life, and the gifts and talents You have given me, and help me to use them all to bring glory to You. In Jesus' name, Amen.

Theme 4

PRAYING FOR OUR FAMILIES

There are characteristics that every family could embrace which will help them develop a lifestyle of learning.

Establishing a lifestyle of learning means that "school" is not limited to 180 days, a particular season, or a traditional schedule. Learning becomes as natural as breathing and is something that brings joy and excitement to life. Something that points to the glory and wonder of God and occurs every day. An activity that not only helps build God's kingdom but also enables us to be salt and light to a lost and dying world.

Let's ask God to help our families develop those qualities which make that lifestyle possible. As believers, we need to develop in ourselves, and help our children learn to:

1. *Maintain healthy relationships*
2. *Develop kindness and generosity towards others*
3. *Think positively*
4. *Use our gifts and talents for the good of others and God's glory*
5. *Place a value and emphasis on learning*
6. *Walk in the light of God's blessing*

Concept 18

Being United with Our Spouse

How good and pleasant it is when God's people live together in unity

Psalm 133:1

Once upon a time, there was a family of four: a husband, his wife, and 2 small children. After they had married, they'd decided together that when the children came, the wife would stay home with them while they were young. A few years after that, baby #2 came along and added even more fun and challenge to the mix :-)

The family moved to a small, rural town and when the kids were old enough, mom trotted child #1 to the public school to begin the education-and-training-for-life process, as all responsible parents do. But after a year or so, the couple decided that this school was not a good fit.

So they moved child #1 to a local private school, and by this time, child #2 was ready as well. They tried hard to make this one work, too, but at the end of the year, they both reached the same decision. This just wasn't working.

The big problem was, they had no other options. Remember how I said they'd moved to a small town? Well, as much as that's a charming visual, it left little to be desired in the education arena. So they found themselves at a crossroads - what to do?

The wife heard about the concept of homeschooling, and talked to some friends who were involved in it, but she was still doubtful. You see, both husband and wife came from families steeped in traditional education system. The wife's dad went to Ivy League schools, and the husband's dad and mom spent their lifetimes working as a middle-school teacher and medical school administrator. After much prayer and research and discussions with those both for and against it, and even after going through a period of being thoroughly convinced she could just never do it, the wife began to consider homeschooling as an option.

Said husband, however, was not sold, despite the dilemma they were facing.

The wife tried convincing the husband, appealing on a variety of levels and using different approaches, to no avail. In prayer one morning, she finally gave up the fight. Considering how it was beginning to affect the family dynamics, she realized this was not a battle in which she should engage. Laying the issue down, she asked the Lord to help her be the best wife and mother she could be, and handle the issue as He saw fit. As is always the case...God came through! Eventually, the husband and wife found themselves on the same page. God brought their hearts in tune with each other and in line with the plan He had for their lives. Over the years, the family grew and experienced their share of bumps and bruises, as we all do, but weathered it all on a united front.

But what happened to the schooling issue, you ask? Well, this story could end in either of 2 ways. I could say that the kids began to blossom in public school, mom went on to be an active, vital part of their classroom, and the family thrived. OR I could say that the couple decided to educate the kids at home, enjoy learning and growing together, and the family thrived.

But, the ending doesn't matter as much as the point I'd like to make.

Ultimately, the most important thing about the way you'll educate your kiddos is that both of you are on the same page.

Moms, even though you may be carrying the lion's share, remember: you can't homeschool in a vacuum. Even if your husband doesn't do a THING in teaching mode, you need his support, his listening ear, and his feedback, knowing he loves your kids as much as you do. When husband and wife are united in their decisions, your family will thrive!

Homeschooling is not a panacea for a bad marriage, for misbehaving kids, or for poor family communications or dynamics. It can be a great opportunity to learn and grow as a family, and to raise great kids who develop their special God-given talents as they become confident, Kingdom-building adults who contribute to society.

Prayer

Dear Lord, sometimes it's so hard to live in unity. The different skills and talents and opinions that we have often create what seems to be insurmountable walls between us!

I see what happens when there is discord in the home. I know how uncomfortable it makes us all, and how disturbing it is for the kids when they feel that tension.

Help me, Jesus, to work hard to be at peace. Fill me with Your Holy Spirit and the fruits that will serve to be a balm to my soul and to others. I pray for unity in our home, Lord, and the ability for me and my husband to see each other's viewpoints, willing to walk in each other's shoes and cherish our uniqueness.

I especially lift up to you this situation *(insert details of what you may be experiencing right now).*

May the unity in our family be a shining example of what You can do when You're at the center of our lives.

I thank You for what You've done and for what You're doing in our lives, in our marriage, and in our home. In Jesus's name I pray, Amen.

Concept 19

Living in Peace Among the Brothers (And Sisters)

Let us therefore make every effort to do what leads to peace and to mutual edification.

Romans 14:19

I don't know if it's like this in your house, but it seems like sometimes all it takes is for ONE of us to wake up on the wrong side of the bed. It not only sets the tone for the day, but leads to discontentment and worse. Moping around leads to grumbling, grumbling leads to picking-on, and picking-on leads to outright bickering and fighting. Allowing or discontentment or boredom to set in, or bad attitudes to persist lead to the same outcome.

Looking back, there were far too many days when I let this happen in our own home. While I realize that I'm not 100% responsible, in my early years of parenting and then homeschooling, I do think that I allowed exhaustion or discouragement to set in, which made it harder to monitor the relationship-meter in our home.

How's the relationship-meter in your home? Do the kids bicker often? Does anyone suffer from discontentment or plain bad attitude? What kind of tapes play over and over in your own head, momma?

"Living together in peace" is a skill. But even with the steeliest of wills, none of us can do this on our own, let alone demand it of our family. It's something that requires the grace and mercy of the Holy Spirit, and the wisdom of the Lord, to accomplish. It requires the consistent practice of forgiveness and letting-go. But oh what a difference it makes - in our lives, in our children's lives, and in our homeschool.

It's definitely something worth working towards and praying about on a daily basis.

Prayer

Oh **Lord**, yes, how good it is when brothers live together in peace!

God, I get so frustrated with myself when I find myself grumbling and complaining. And even more so when I see what happens when that bad attitude spills over into my relationship with the kids, my husband and others. I see how different the day is when there is fighting and bickering. And I see on my children's faces how their hearts break when there is no peace - and that in turn breaks my own.

Today, Lord, I invite you into our home, in fact, I beg Your presence in this situation *(share details here)*, because I know that where You are there is perfect peace. I know we will still have quarrels and disagreements, but help us to seek You in those times so we can move on quickly to forgiveness and then...peace.

Thank you today, and evermore, for your promise of peace to those who love and follow You. Keep us in Your Word and Your peace as we grow in love and obedience each day. And I ask this all in Jesus' name, Amen.

Concept 20

Being Kind and Generous to Others

But when the kindness and love of God our Savior appeared, he saved us, not because of righteous things we had done, but because of his mercy.

Titus 3:4-5a

Kindness is a quality that is sorely lacking in our society today. I haven't done any scientific studies, but I know in my personal experience there has been a direct correlation between wisdom and kindness in our own home.

With two young children, we lived in a city far from both sets of parents, my husband worked long hours establishing his construction business, and we knew no one in town. Add to that the fact that my own step-mother wasn't exactly the maternal type and had never raised little ones herself, and I felt like I was floundering in rough "new motherhood" waters.

With little wisdom on what the Bible had to say about parenting, when stress or lack of sleep hit me, kindness wasn't even to be found in my universe.

Thankfully, God intervened and sent me some wonderful friends who mentored and loved me into becoming a better parent. Who taught me the value and necessity of handling stress so as not to take it out on my kids. Who taught me the importance of modeling kindness and how to encourage it in them.

There is no understating the importance of kindness in our own homes, and it's effect as it spills over into our homeschools. When we think of others' needs above our own. When we offer undeserved grace. When we choose to respond with a quiet word - or sometimes with none at all. When we reach out with a hug or a kind gesture or a "Hey, I'm on your side, sweetie!", we sow seeds of kindness.

Nobody is more kind than our Heavenly Father. In His kindness, He sent His Son to a world that did not ask for mercy and certainly did not deserve it. His love is the perfect model of kindness for us to follow.

Let's shoot for that model today - and encourage our children to do the same.

Then step back and watch our homes and our homeschools be transformed!

Prayer

Lord God, there is no one like You! Thank You for the extreme model of kindness that You show us in Your Word. I want to be more like You, Jesus. Let me humbly learn from the kindness that You've shown me, and seek to imitate that in all my actions today.

Help my words, and even the tone of them; help my actions and my gestures; help my thoughts and attitudes, all reflect kindness today. And even where discipline is concerned, give me wisdom to know how to be firm without being harsh and mean-spirited. To know the difference between childishness and foolishness, especially in this situation *(talk about something specific here)*. To know how to discipline in love and kindness.

Thank You for Your help, and Your own kindness towards me and those around me. This day I ask that You'd give me Your Holy

Spirit to fill me with that kindness, especially in this area *(talk about something specific here)*. And in doing so, make me more and more like You in every way. In Jesus' name, Amen.

Concept 21

Thinking Positively

Finally, brothers and sisters, whatever is true, whatever is noble,
whatever is right, whatever is pure,
whatever is lovely, whatever is admirable—if anything is excellent or
praiseworthy—think about such things.

PHILIPPIANS 4:8

I was once called a "Pollyanna" by a very close friend of mine.

She meant well, at least I really think she did.

She was referring to a tendency I've been cultivating over the years. It hasn't been easy, but I've worked at finding something beneficial from those trying, or even negative, situations in which I sometimes find myself.

- How to pay that big property tax bill at the end of the year? Time for me to ask God for wisdom and practice trusting in His provision.
- Having a misunderstanding with a friend? Here's a perfect opportunity to pray for peace, softened hearts toward each other, and understanding and healing.
- Behavior problems with the kids? Maybe God is asking me to look at my own heart, too, and see if there are any

parallels. Now might be the time to put away my pride and seek wise counsel in this area.

- Hurting from the loss of a loved one? Have an increased need for rest or peace? Feeling anxious? These are perfect occasions to bring my needs to the Father. Perhaps they are even events orchestrated in His plan to bring me to a closer and deeper relationship with Him.

At the time, the name "Pollyanna" stung. But after I paused, and gave it some thought, I went to God with it, asking Him if I was being too naïve and looking at the world through rose-colored glasses.

But in my heart, all I heard was this: think on **Me**. Come to **Me**. ***My*** opinion is all that matters.

Something else worth thinking about today.

Prayer

Loving Father, I greet You this morning with questions on my heart. I look around and see the pain and devastation in the world, and I have to wonder why it exists. I even consider the struggles in my own life and wonder how and why You allow them to happen, and to what benefit they could possibly lead *(insert some specifics here)*.

Why is it so easy to focus on the negatives?

Lord, give me fresh eyes this day. Help me see the opportunities to comfort and minister to those in pain. Help me use heartache as opportunities to run to You and seek Your comfort and peace. Help me look at situations that bring confusion or pain to my humanness with a new mind and a new heart. Help me see the potential benefit in whatever happens to me today. Help me find the truth, and think on what is right and pure and praiseworthy in Your world and in my life.

And help me - today and each day - encourage my family and those in my path to do the same. In Jesus' name, Amen.

Concept 22

Using Their Talents to Bless God

Let the message of Christ dwell among you richly as you teach and admonish one another with all wisdom through psalms, hymns, and songs from the Spirit, singing to God with gratitude in your hearts.

COLOSSIANS 3:16

Music. I love music. And my kids love music. As a matter of fact, most of my memories are accompanied by a soundtrack. For as long as I can remember, music has been an integral part of my life.

Classical music was often softly playing in the background during our early homeschool years, and we all enjoyed listening to (my secret favorite) classic rock of the 60's, 70's and 80's in the car or during lunch, as they grew older.

And in that same vein, music is important in my worship. While I'm not about to choose or leave a church based on the musical style, there are some types of music that move me more than others.

Both science and the Bible back up those feelings. As a Music Therapy student in college, I studied the various emotional, psychological and physical reactions that music provokes. These days, reading Scripture, I also see the spiritual influence of music, how it is both a cause for and effect of worship.

Whether or not you find yourself especially moved by tunes, Scripture does encourage us to teach and admonish (encourage) each other, and express gratitude to God from our hearts. Music is often part of the experience. Touching our hearts and emotions deeply, music springs from the soul, rich and sincere.

It's important to teach our children to develop gratitude to God, and be bold leaders ("teach and admonish each other"). Oftentimes, they will be moved to song, especially when they're young. Help them to hold on to that raw and true emotion. Help them to use it to worship and communicate with God. Help them to use the skills and talents they have to bless and benefit those around them, so that "the message of Christ dwell(s) among (them) richly!"

Prayer

Loving Father, thank You for the gift and blessing of music. Knowing that it springs from You, knowing that the angels in heaven praise You with it all day, reading about how Your people used it lavishly in ceremony and worship, it comes as no surprise to me that music touches our hearts. I ask You today, Lord, to fill our hearts with music. Fill our hearts and minds that songs that give You praise and express our gratitude for all You are and all You do. In Jesus' precious name, Amen.

Concept 23

Praying for Their Future

For I know the plans I have for you," declares the Lord, "plans to prosper you and not to harm you, plans to give you hope and a future. Then you will call on me and come and pray to me, and I will listen to you. You will seek me and find me when you seek me with all your heart. I will be found by you," declares the Lord

JEREMIAH 29:11

I couldn't believe we were here - graduation day had finally come! Well, actually, it had come around again for the 4th time in our family. I moved through the day in a haze: waking up, preparing breakfast, packing the car up with our post-graduation party items, heading over to the church where our ceremony was being held... There were a dozen other graduates there, too: young adults whom I had watched grow for much of their lives. It was truly surreal.

And as always, this event led me to think back on my other kids, and even friends of theirs to whom our family was close. Some were doing well, yes, but others were struggling, some in school, others unsure of what path to take in life. Some had left the faith of their childhood, exploring unhealthy activities or lifestyles. In my head I know that overcoming challenges and problems makes for a stronger and more resilient and capable adult. Yet, there is a part of me (and maybe you, too!) that wants my teen's life to go smoothly. To have barely a bump in the road. To know what they want to do for their future and then move ahead and "git 'er done".

It's important for us to remember that the words of encouragement found in Jeremiah 29 were delivered to people who were living in exile. The Jewish nation had been carried into Babylon (enemy territory) and were not exactly having a party.

In the midst of living with the challenges and problems of life in a foreign and hostile land, God reminds them of His promise. He goes on to assure them that He will carry them all back to the place from which they left - and He makes good on that promise.

We can and should pray that over and for our children, too. No matter where they are; no matter what "foreign land" or difficult situation or outright painful place any of us are in, if we seek His face, He will deliver and lead us.

Let's be diligent about praying for our kids, especially as they grow into the teens years and adulthood. God's word never returns void. And let's start today - if you haven't already - praying for their futures!

Prayer

Lord God, I know that you love my child even more than I, I know that you have plans for his or her future, as well as my own. Right now, Lord, this particular situation *(include details here)* looks pretty dismal. Help me to get my eyes off the situation, and on You. I lift up my teen's life - their present situation and their future - to Your hands. Help me to trust You more and more each day as you mold us all into Your image. Help me to remember that everything that happens today and in their future comes as no surprise to You, and has been filtered through Your loving hands. Lord, bring to fruition everything you have planned from the beginning of time for my child. Bring them a job or career that is personally fulfilling and enables them to bless others. Raise up a spouse and family that they can serve and love. And turn their hearts to You, Lord, so that no matter what tomorrow brings, they may lift Your name and love You through it all.

I thank You for all You have done, are doing, and will do in my children's lives...in Jesus' name, Amen.

Concept 24

Living Out the Blessing

For we are God's handiwork, created in Christ Jesus to do good works, which God prepared in advance for us to do.

Ephesians 2:10

One of the things we did right as parents was to have a Blessing Service* for our kids in their 13th year. I encourage every parent I meet to craft their own version of this. When we began planning our very first one, we had no idea that we were setting the stage for a deep and meaningful family tradition. Given the importance of words as outlined in Scripture, we believe it is important to have an aspect of the spoken word as well. The resulting event became a festive occasion the rest of our children anticipated and enjoyed as well.

The motivation behind it was two-fold: to provide a spiritual "stepping stone" to launch our teens into young adulthood, and to encourage them to grow into God's plan for their lives. Yes, to some, 13 seemed a bit young for that. But in our experience, the event resulted in a visible jump in maturity and growth. Though we set a high bar, our teens sought to reach it!

In these confusing times, our teens need to know when they have arrived at Biblical adulthood, remember the support and guidance available from loving friends and family, and be encouraged to grow into the plan God has created for them before the beginning of time.

If your teen is floundering, or to encourage him even if he is not, ask the Lord if He would have you celebrate and support him (or her!) in this way.

*see the Resources section for more information about crafting your own event

Prayer

Heavenly Father, because You are the perfect parent, help me to seek Your face and discover how You would have us parent our precious blessings. You brought creation into being through Your Word. Lord, help me to speak blessings into our own children's lives this day and every day, especially in these areas *(detail areas they're struggling with right now).*

Grow me more and more to be like You, and as I lift my teens into Your hands, grow them more and more to be like You as well. May the words of my mouth and the meditation of my heart be ever pleasing to You, Lord… (Psalm 19:14) And I ask this all in Jesus' name, Amen

Theme 5

PRAYING FOR OUR HOMESCHOOL

Even though our lives often feel like they revolve around teaching and parenting the kids, God would say otherwise. There is not only so much more in life, there is something even more important to remember: everything we do is to be in obedience to ***Him,*** *and our ultimate goal in life is to give* ***Him*** *glory.*

But He ***has*** *given us an amazing blessing through the gift of our children, and the privilege of being able to educate and disciple them. That aspect of our lives, and all that it entails, is important to Him as well.*

Now let's "laser" our prayers in on that area.

Concept 25

Developing a Lifestyle of Learning

Buy the truth and do not sell it -
Wisdom, instruction and insight as well.

Proverbs 23:23

Every January, I find two things happening:

1. I get tons of sales calls (yup, even on my cell phone!) from people trying to get me to buy...insurance, cars (can you believe it?!), business loans. Stuff I'd ne-ver buy from someone soliciting me over the phone. It makes me wonder why this is even a business model...until I realize that somebody must be buying this stuff or they wouldn't be making these calls!

2. And I also see lots of blog posts about changing up curricula or mid-year tweaking, and ads for "new", "improved", "must-try" programs or classes that promise to be just the ticket to recharge your homeschool.

Which gets me to thinking: what am I spending my money on? What am I spending my energies on?

You know the saying: "It's either time or money." It means that, at the end of the day, everything has a cost. For my homeschool, I know it's very easy to be attracted to the latest/greatest product or book and either buy what I can't afford, or become dissatisfied and discontent with what I'm already doing.

Neither option presents itself as a preferable lifestyle.

We have to be very intentional about developing a lifestyle of learning. But when that concept is in the forefront, it makes all the difference in what we spend our money on, and where we spend our time. It serves as a filter through which we can choose "the best" from all "the good" out there. Learning becomes exciting, and not drudgery. Learning curves become challenges, rather than things to dread.

So before you buy anything else this year - whether it's for your homeschool or your home in general - try looking at it through this filter, too.

You will, of course, need to spend some time in the Word. But remember that God gives wisdom freely to those who ask!

So let's buy the truth with our time this morning...and seek God first!

Prayer

Father God, I come to You this day with a heart that is heavy and full of woe. Lord, I see so many who value ease and pleasure at any cost and fail to see the treasure of hard work and growth. I know You value my character over my comfort. Help me to have that same perspective and value wisdom, seek Your truth, and gain greater insight in the process.

I so want my life, and our children's lives, to further Your kingdom and bring glory to Your name in all we say and do. As we start a new day, help us to feel Your presence and follow Your guidance as we learn and grow together. I especially need Your guidance regarding *(insert your own need here)*. I ask this all in the wonderful name of Jesus, Amen.

Concept 26

Choosing Methods and Materials

Fix these words of mine in your hearts and minds; tie them as symbols on your hands and bind them on your foreheads.
Teach them to your children, talking about them when you sit at home and when you walk along the road, when you lie down and when you get up. Write them on the doorframes of your houses and on your gates

DEUTERONOMY 11:18-20

At certain times each year, many homeschoolers are recognizing that their curricula may not be "working" quite as they anticipated. Perhaps your child is encountering a stumbling block in math, or not quite getting a concept in science. Maybe you find yourself nagging them to get their history projects done, or keep up with their language arts assignments, or study Spanish.

I've been there and done that, and let me tell you…it may be the curriculum, but it might not be!

Here's the deal: there IS no perfect program of study out there. But let me ask you to think about this: have you prayed over your homeschool curriculum choices lately? That might seem like a funny question, and I have to admit that there have been times I have not, whether it was because I felt rushed or acted like a kid in a candy store. You know, falling for the latest new and shiny and great-looking book or product or system. But if you're dreading Mondays...if things aren't going like you'd anticipated last fall...well, maybe it's time to try something new.

I'm not necessarily talking about changing up what you're doing, but how about we ask the Lord about it before doing anything else?

Prayer

Lord God, today I find myself facing yet another Monday. I want to be excited and encouraged about the days to unfold before me, and yet I have some misgivings. Not everything is turning out as I had planned. Or hoped. And God, today I'm not sure if it's me or my curriculum choices! I realize that I don't always ask You about them, tho; that I need to break new ground here. So Father, I'm asking you today, and for always, to lead me to the best materials for my children. I know each one is unique, but there are oh-so-many learning choices available that it sometimes makes my head spin! Please help me to choose well, help me to know what will best meet my children's needs and prepare them to serve You well. *(Ask for guidance regarding a specific product or opportunity you're considering.)* And when I fail to seek You first, in all my purchases, please forgive me and use my mistakes to teach us both. I lift up our homeschool to you, and ask You to be Lord of the process and the product. In Jesus' name, Amen.

Concept 27

Harnessing the Power of Love

If I speak in the tongues of men or of angels, but do not have love,
I am only a resounding gong or a clanging cymbal.
If I have the gift of prophecy and can fathom all mysteries and all knowledge,
and if I have a faith that can move mountains, but do not have love,
I am nothing.

1 Corinthians 13:1-2

When I was growing up, my mom used to tell me "you catch more flies with honey than with vinegar." She was trying to teach me how to deal with people who were being mean to me.

But we shouldn't stop being sweet as honey in those situations; acting in a loving manner to those around us is Biblical. And yes, it's hard.

I don't know about you, but these days I sometimes find it's easier to be sweet as sugar to strangers and even those I don't like, than it is to be considerate and kind to my own family. I mean, they're supposed to love me no matter what, right? They should know that

I love them, even when I'm not acting that way. And can't they tell when I'm having a bad day, or in a bad mood, and not take things so personally?

Of course, if the shoe were on the other foot, I have to ask myself, would I be so understanding?

Most likely the answer is "no".

I need to take that lesson to heart. I need to remember that without love, it doesn't matter who I am, or what I've done or am doing, or what my "intentions" are. People won't remember what I've done for them as much as they'll remember how they felt while I'm around. That includes my husband and my kiddos.

Starting with me, I can refocus a bad day on a dime. With Jesus' love and joy as my strength, I can move the "mountains" of a bad attitude or the beginnings of a lousy homeschool day…

Let's try this together: the next time you find the day starting out on the wrong foot, or when you've found yourself making a misstep in your relationships, pause, ask God to fill you with His love and spill it over to those around you.

Then step back and watch what happens!

Prayer

Loving Father, when I think of the reaches of Your love, I am absolutely overwhelmed. I know that some days it's all I can do to just put up with the situations I find myself in, let alone love deeply as a wife or mom or friend.

Lord, help me to meditate on the richness of Your love for me and for those around me. Let those thoughts, and Your Holy Spirit, change me from within so that I can be more and more like You. Let me become a reflection of Your love to those around me, and an agent for change as I do so. I so long to be all You've created me to be, and as I teach and disciple the children You've blessed me with *(mention your kids by name)*, help them to grow into whom You've created them to be, as well. I know that on my own I can do none of this, but Lord - ***You*** can!

Help our homeschool go beyond books and learning what is temporal, and transform it into a tool of love through which Your will be done! In Jesus' name, I pray, Amen.

Concept 28

Establishing Order and Self-Discipline

But everything should be done in a fitting and orderly way.

1 Corinthians 14:40

A **few years into homeschooling**, my husband began to notice an extreme lack of, shall we say "order" in our home, when he would occasionally come home for lunch.

Initially, he didn't say anything.

He would greet us all, spend a few minutes with each of the kids, and then we'd all dig in and eat together.

But one day, he pulled me aside and asked me what my home-school day usually looked like.

"Well," I responded, "the kids usually get up around 7, we have a quick breakfast and get started by 8 or so. By lunchtime, we're all ready for a break, so we enjoy when you come home to eat with us."

"But I mean, what does your morning "look like?" He pushed even further, "How do you order your day?"

"Well, I like to be flexible," I said proudly. "This way we're ready in case some impromptu learning opportunity comes up!"

After further discussion, he said something that stuck with me forever after. "But you can't be "flexible" if you have nothing to be flexible from…" Or, put another way, if you have no order to start with, all you're doing is pushing through chaos each day.

While the kids were young, that didn't bother me. But as they grew older, I realized the wisdom in that statement. After all, through the years, the kids and I have walked through enough Bible stories together to realize how even God Himself is a God of order. Not only did He first create the concept of order, but then He created the universe using that same concept. He is a God of process and plans, and His are all good.

To this day I consider not only our homeschool, but my own life, as a process. I encourage my kids to do this as well in their own lives, although I realize I ultimately have very little say in how or even if they will apply this to themselves.

It's not about having a legalistic schedule, but it IS about having a plan, a purpose, and living an intentional life.

Prayer

Lord, I come to you this morning, knowing that You have both a purpose and a plan for my life, as well as my children's, and ask You to give me a clear vision of them, especially regarding *(insert here an issue or person that you're concerned about)*. I know You have the future in Your hands, and only You ultimately know what path we will take and the best way to get there.

But I ask you, this day, to make our time count. Lead our steps in an orderly fashion, a journey crafted to bring You glory in everything we do and say. A journey that will not only help us know You better each day, but will also make us more and more like You as the days progress.

I thank you, Father, for all You have done and are doing and will do in our lives, in the precious name of Your Son, Jesus, Amen.

Concept 29

Accepting God's Provision

Give us this day our daily bread.

Matthew 6:11

H**igh school was rearing its ugly head.** My oldest child was in 8th grade, and we were coming quickly upon the high school years. I was terrified, to say the least.

Besides "the basics," there were subjects like biology and chemistry lab courses, foreign language, advanced math (gulp!). How could I EVER teach those courses? The public school situation in our community hadn't taken a turn for the better and there was NO way we could afford a private or Christian school, either.

What were we going to do?

That was a huge concern, and yes, I'll admit, worry. But our homeschool years have been full of those, and lesser examples. Times that we found ourselves struggling with questions such as: Where will the money come from? How will they get experience in __________? What will we do to handle this subject? Are they getting enough training in __________?

When I say homeschooling has been a faith-builder for me, these are the situations to which I refer. Each time, God has come through for our family. The cool thing is that it has never been in ways we could have foreseen, or in ways that we ever could have planned on our own.

God provides, friends, never before it's necessary…but always on time!

Prayer

God of all time, this morning I come to you with yet another situation that I'm not in control of but I am worried about or stressed-out over. *(Name it here.)* I thank You, Lord, that You are Lord of our homeschool and our lives, and I know that this situation has not come as a surprise to You. God, I'm asking You today to give me the peace that passes all understanding and to help me trust in You and Your provision. You've said in Your Word that you don't leave Your people forsaken or in want (Psalm 37:25). Help me to know that You will provide for our needs, whether it's daily bread, a learning program or plan that will help our children, or the finances to cover our bills. I know that at the end of the day, Father, You are enough, You are all we need, and You are the author and finisher of our faith and our lives.

Thank You, Lord, for providing for all our needs, those we know of and even those we are yet unaware of, and doing it in Your perfect way, and in Your perfect timing. We thank You even now for the answers that are yet unseen. In Jesus' name, Amen.

Concept 30

Establishing Traditions

Follow my example, as I follow the example of Christ.
I praise you for remembering me in everything
and for holding to the traditions
just as I passed them on to you.

1 CORINTHIANS 11:1-2

My eldest daughter asked us to join her for Thanksgiving that year. It may not sound like a big deal, except when you understand that this would be the first time in 31 years of marriage that I would not be hosting the holiday. But it was a lovely time, and it was lots of fun helping out in her kitchen. We had a wonderful holiday.

This is the same daughter who asked us to change the day we celebrate Passover one year, so she could be a part of the festivities with us. We timed it during her break at the school in South Korea where she taught ESL, and she flew back to the States for that special occasion.

Traditions. These are some of them in our family, and it is truly a blessing to this mother's heart to see her children treasure them.

The same is true when my husband and I see their love for the Lord. To know and see that our children walk with Him is probably the greatest "tradition" of them all. There is absolutely no substitute for a relationship with Jesus.

While you may not necessarily teach that in your homeschool, you can surely model it. And I pray that you will model it for your children every day, whether "in" or "out" of school.

Prayer

Father God, I am so grateful for traditions: those events and activities that we do as a family that keep us bound together to each other, and together to You. Whether they are special times that our children treasure, or sacred times to worship You together, I ask that You would always keep them significant and special in our lives.

Help us, Lord, not to be legalistic in what we do or say or how we act, but use those times to make our relationships stronger, to learn more about each other and even ourselves, and to celebrate the people and situations, and even the world, that You have provided for us.

Thank You for all the time You allow us to have, and help us to give it all back to You… In Jesus' name, Amen.

Concept 31
Being Obedient

But the Lord replied, "Have you any right to be angry?"

JONAH 4:4

(YOU CAN READ THE WHOLE BOOK ON YOUR OWN)

The book of Jonah is short (4 chapters) and can be interpreted in many ways. My study Bible talks about it as a foreshadowing of Jesus' death and resurrection, but here I'd like to point out what it teaches about obedience.

Throughout the story, we see Jonah set on doing what he wants. First, of course, heading in the opposite direction of where God wanted him to go (we never do that, do we?), and then pouting when things didn't go his way (chapter 4). As a matter of fact, he eventually gets so frustrated that he directs all his emotions towards a plant, something that springs from the earth and soon fades away. God's response, of course, focuses on the bigger picture, pointing out that His heart was intent on the salvation of the thousands of people in the city: His creations and souls with eternal futures

Jonah argues with God, like we and our children sometimes do. And today's focus is that we would **all** become set on obeying Him:

- not ignoring Him or developing "selective hearing"
- not acknowledging His Word and commandments without accepting them for ourselves
- not accepting them, perhaps, but obeying with resentment.

True obedience is quick, complete and joyful. That quality is an important characteristic for our children and ourselves! As we talked about in previous chapters, it's important to model it for them in our own lives, and then require it from them in our home and homeschool.

Prayer

Lord, I confess to you today the times I have not modeled obedience to You. The times that I may have done what You'd asked with a grumbling spirit. The times that I may have insisted on my own way. Father God, I want to do better! My heart is so thankful for all Your blessings, and for Who You are. I rejoice in the compassion and mercy You've shown me and my family. And I want the peace that comes from resting in Your truth, Your wisdom, Your protection, and provision. Today, and every day forward, I pray that I may move closer and closer to trusting and obeying You always. Be present in my life and this day. Speak to me as only You can so that I may hear Your direction in my life, and obey You without reservation. I pray this for my children, as well. In Jesus' name, Amen.

Resources

Here's the list of Scriptures used during the course of this book:

Psalm 66:16-20
Daniel 9:20-23
Psalm 147:1-6
Lamentations 2:19
Psalm 51:10-12
Isaiah 57:15
Habakkuk 3: 17-18
Proverbs 1:7
1 Corinthians 2:4-6
James 1:5, Luke 11:9-10
Proverbs 1:32-33
Philippians 1:9
Colossians 1:9-10
James 3:17
Proverbs 23:23
Deuteronomy 11:18-20
1 Corinthians 13:1-2
1 Corinthians 14:40
Matthew 6:11
1 Corinthians 11:1-2
The Book of Jonah
Psalm 133:1
Romans 14:19
Titus 3:4-5a
Philippians 4:8
Colossians 3:16
Proverbs 24:14, Jeremiah 29:11
Ephesians 2:10, Psalm 19:14

Genesis 1:26; Luke 12:7
Romans 12:2
Psalm 139:14

Download the FREE journal for your own notes as you work through this book: https://breakthroughhomeschooling.com/devojournal

Listen to the "Prayers for a Lifetime of Learning" podcast on iTunes!

About the Author

Pat Fenner is making the most of her "retired homeschool mom" status. She encourages and inspires others as they continue the journey through the high school years at her blog BreakthroughHomeschooling. After almost 25 years of home-educating her five children (now mostly grown), she also helps moms find meaning and purpose in the "post-homeschooling" stage of life as she herself navigates and explores this new territory. She anticipates finding time to work in the garden again someday, lovin' on her new granddaughter (and future grands!), and enjoys nothing more than getting together with a friend over a hot cup of coffee.

Made in United States
Orlando, FL
10 July 2022

19591551R00065

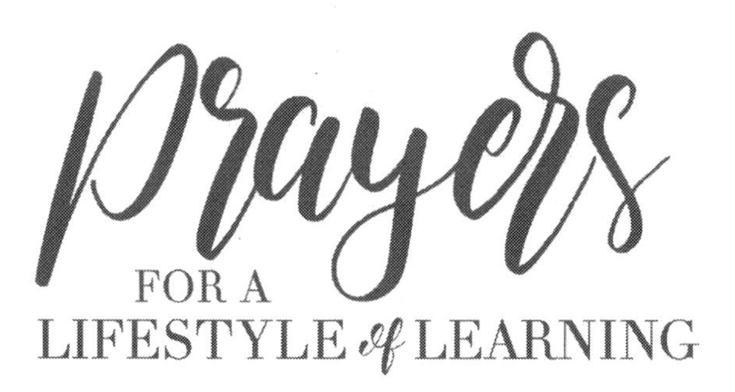
Prayers
FOR A
LIFESTYLE of LEARNING